EARTH*ROCKS!*
CANYONS

BY SARA GILBERT

CREATIVE EDUCATION • CREATIVE PAPERBACKS

Published by Creative Education and Creative Paperbacks
P.O. Box 227, Mankato, Minnesota 56002
Creative Education and Creative Paperbacks are
imprints of The Creative Company
www.thecreativecompany.us

Design and production by Chelsey Luther
Art direction by Rita Marshall
Printed in the United States of America

Photographs by Alamy (Tetyana Kochneva, June Morrissey, Nature Picture Library, Maxim Petrichuk, Sara Winter), Dreamstime (TMarchev, Dmitry Vinogradov), Getty Images (Arctic-Images, Matteo Colombo, Anna Gorin, Gordon Wiltsie), iStockphoto (4kodiak, Spondylolithesis), Spoon Graphics (Chris Spooner)

Library of Congress Cataloging-in-Publication Data
Names: Gilbert, Sara.
Title: Canyons / Sara Gilbert.
Series: Earth Rocks!
Includes bibliographical references and index.
Summary: An elementary exploration of canyons, focusing on the geological evidence that helps explain how and where they form and spotlighting famous examples, such as Arizona's Grand Canyon.
Identifiers: ISBN 978-1-60818-891-8 (hardcover) / ISBN 978-1-62832-507-2 (pbk) / ISBN 978-1-56660-943-2 (eBook)

This title has been submitted for CIP processing under
LCCN 2017937617.

CCSS: RI.1.1, 2, 4, 5, 6, 7; RI.2.2, 5, 6, 7, 10; RI.3.1, 5, 7, 8; RF.1.1, 3, 4; RF.2.3, 4

First Edition HC 9 8 7 6 5 4 3 2 1
　　　　　PBK 9 8 7 6 5 4 3 2

*Pictured on cover: Altyn-Emel National Park, Kazakhstan (top);
Antelope Canyon, Arizona (bottom)*

TABLE OF CONTENTS

CARVED EARTH

Standing at the edge of a canyon takes your breath away! It looks like a deep trail has been cut into the earth. You are looking at layers of rocks that may be millions of years old.

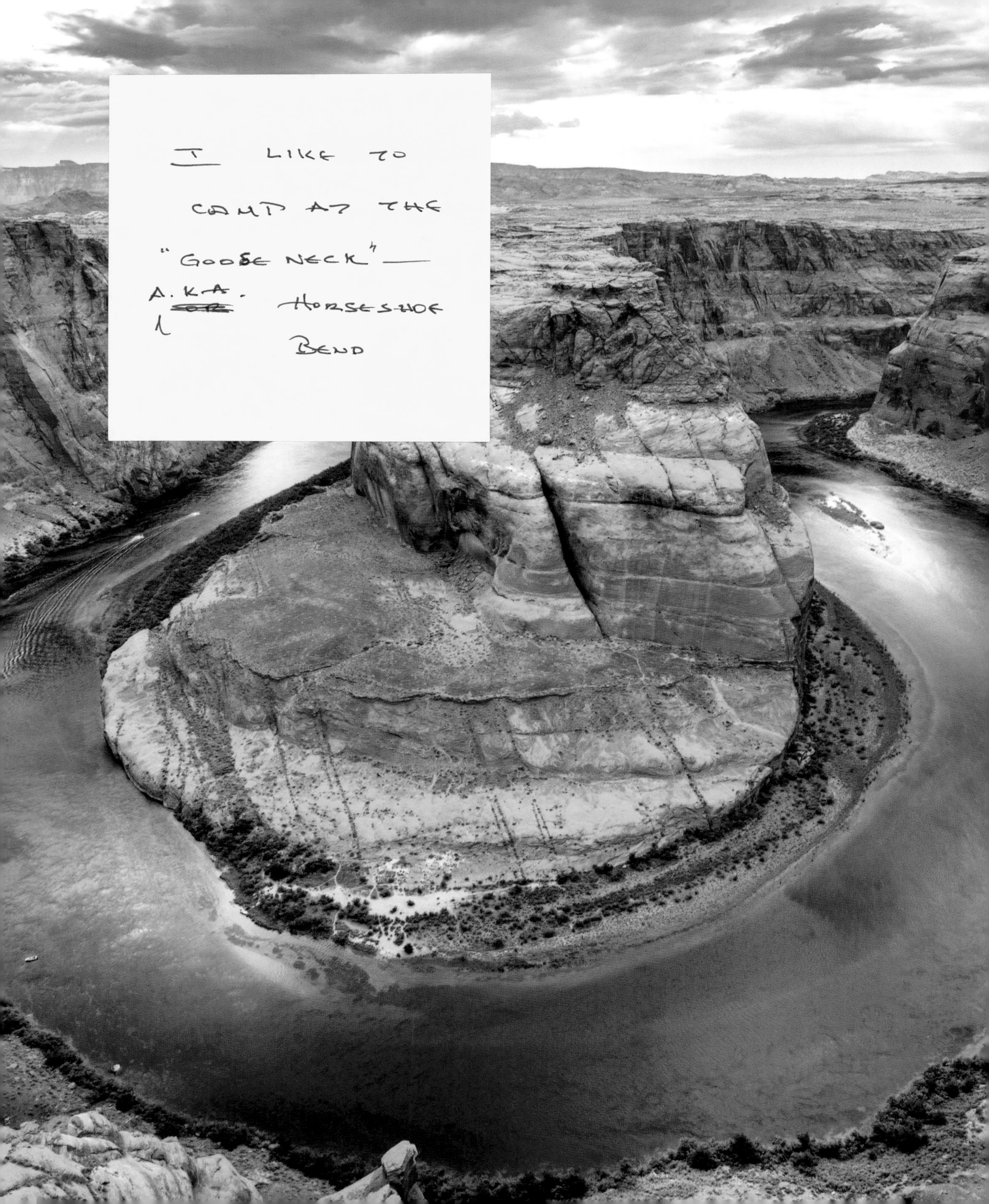
I LIKE TO
CAMP AT THE
"GOOSE NECK" —
A.K.A. HORSESHOE
BEND

LIMESTONE

WALLS OF ROCK

A canyon is a deep, narrow valley. It runs between two cliffs. It is carved into hard rocks like granite, sandstone, and limestone.

A canyon can be more than a mile deep and several miles wide. Sometimes a river runs through it.

RUNNING WATER

Most canyons are formed by **erosion**. Over time, rivers wear away layers of rock. Wind can form canyons, too. It blows softer soil away.

ANTELOPE CANYON

UTAH

Sometimes, canyons form because water freezes in the cracks between rocks. The ice breaks the rocks apart.

slot canyon

ANTELOPE CANYON

box canyon

CORRIESHALLOCH GORGE

river canyon

GLEN CANYON

submarine canyon

SILFRA CANYON

KINDS OF CANYONS

Every canyon looks different.

Narrow canyons with smooth walls are called slot canyons. Box canyons have three sides. Underwater canyons are called **submarine** canyons.

CANYONS ARE EVERYWHERE

Canyons can be found on almost every **continent**. Anywhere water flows, a canyon can be formed. They are more common in hot, dry areas.

WHITE CANYON, EGYPT

YARLUNG TSANGPO GRAND CANYON, TIBET

FAMOUS CANYONS

The deepest canyon in the world is in Tibet. It is 18,000 feet (5,486 m) deep!

GRAND CANYON

The Grand Canyon is in Arizona. It is 277 miles (446 km) long! About 5 million people visit it every year. You can hike in the canyon or see it from a bus or helicopter. It makes a great family vacation!

It takes a day of humping to get to the bottom and back in one day. The temperature gradient is extreme: it might be cold at the top rim, but the base is hot! So bring lots of water & good shoes.

ACTIVITY: MAKE A MINI CANYON

Materials

Sand

Food coloring

Clear food storage container

5 sandwich bags

Water

Scissors

1. Fill each sandwich bag with sand.

2. Add several drops of food coloring to each bag and shake for a minute. The colored sand is for the different layers of rock.

3. Pour one bag of sand into the food container at a time. Make even layers across the bottom. Look through the side of the container to see the different layers!

4. Fill one of the empty sandwich bags with water. Use your scissors to cut a small hole in one corner of the bag. Let the water pour into your sand and make a river.

5. Tip the container to help the water flow. What happens to the sand as the water runs through it?

GLOSSARY

continent: one of the seven main land masses on Earth

erosion: the process of slowly being worn away

submarine: existing under the surface of the sea

READ MORE

Hanson, Erik. *Canyons*. New York: Chelsea House, 2007.

Nadeau, Isaac. *Canyons*. New York: PowerKids Press, 2006.

WEBSITES

National Geographic: Canyons
http://science.nationalgeographic.com/science/earth/surface-of-the-earth/canyons-article/
Learn more about how canyons are formed and what they look like.

World Landforms: Canyon
http://worldlandforms.com/landforms/canyon/
See pictures of canyons and learn more about canyon characteristics.

Note: Every effort has been made to ensure that any websites listed above were active at the time of publication and suitable for children. However, because of the nature of the Internet, it is impossible to guarantee that these sites will remain active indefinitely or that their contents will not be altered.

INDEX